'Doctor, I keep thinking people are ignoring me.' 'Next!'

To the man who invented zero. Thanks for nothing.

What do they call the Italian Bigfoot? Spaghetti squach!

TV is called a medium because anything well done is rare.

I wanted to become a photographer, but I lost focus!

This year, there will be a really special convention for the Fibonacci Club. It is supposed to be as big as the last two combined!

The royal family moved into my neighborhood. They live Tudors down.

My friend came from a broken home. His Dad was a shocker at DIY.

Son: 'What exactly is an acorn?' Dad: 'Well, in a nutshell, it's an oak tree!'

What did the science teacher climb? A chemi-tree

If a rabbit raced a cabbage, which would win? The cabbage because it's a head.

How did the baguette celebrate graduating from school? It made french toast.

When Magnesium and Oxygen started dating, I was like, "OMG!"

I've got an eating disorder. I go coffee first, then pudding, and then the main course.

Why are ducks bad doctors? Because they're all quacks.

It's really hard to play basketball against Garbagemen. They talk so much trash.

Did you hear about the eyeglasses maker who moved his shop to an island off Alaska and is now known as an optical Aleutian?

Dad says middle age is when the glass is still half full. Mom says that's true, but soon, his teeth will be floating in it!

My neighbor is a witch, and I wish she would get her vehicle a muffler; all I hear every morning is BRRRROOM BRRRRROOM.

Dad says he's only pushing forty. Mom says he's clinging on to it for dear life.

I don't often tell dad jokes... cause he's going deaf.

You got hit by a rental car? Yeah. Hertz.

What did the bowl say to her child? Be responsi-bowl

Why Did The Chicken Get Sent Off? For persistent fowl play!

What was the most ground-breaking invention in human history? The shovel

Why did Dad get fired from the banana factory? He kept throwing away the bent ones!

How do teacups count? Thir-tea-eight, thir-tea-nine, four-tea!

Why did the squid cross the ocean? To get to the other tide.

The only way prisoners can call each other is on cell phones.

Why do hockey players make terrible comedians? They always end up in the penalty box for their punchlines!

Are snails faster without their shells? No, they're more sluggish!

So I bought this DVD, and in the Extras it said 'Deleted Scenes. When I had a look, there was nothing there.

I used to be a motorcycle courier. Boy, those things are heavy!.

Angel: We need to save
God: I Noah guy.

Where do sloths love to go
to eat? Any rest-aurant.

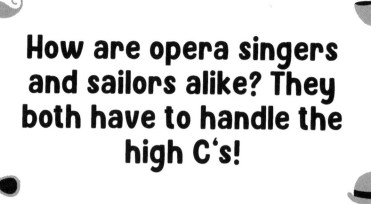

How are opera singers
and sailors alike? They
both have to handle the
high C's!

What's Irish and stays out all night? Patio Furniture

What is extremely loud, salty, expensive, crunchy, and supported by a group of scientists? A rocket chip.

When I was interviewing for a new job, the recruiter asked where I thought I'd see myself in five years. I suspect I'll still be using mirrors for that.

What should a man do when he has a lot of problems? Open a mathematics book. It has many solutions!

My favorite rock group actually doesn't sing at all, but they've got four great members. Have you heard of Mount Rushmore?

What days do fish dislike the most? Fry-Day

The fisherman offered me his catch for free one day, but I didn't take it. It seemed a bit fishy to me.

Which singer is the fastest at stitching clothes? Taylor Swift!

The reason why shipbuilders never galvanize ships is because that would make them zinc.

Why do people always say "break a leg" to actors? Because there is always a cast!

I'd look good with a bow made of wood around my neck. Wooden tie?

The best jokes about oranges have a tang of truth in them.

My son is a redhead, and he always makes the worst sandwiches. He insists on using gingerbread.

Dad says he's still broad-minded and narrow-waisted. Mom says soon those will be changing places.

Why was the archaeologist upset? His job was in ruins!

My boss said to me, 'This is the fifth time you've come into work late this week. Do you know what this means?' 'Yes,' I replied, 'it's Friday!'

The bathroom sink is red because my mom colored her hair. It looks like someone dyed in there.

Why did Microsoft PowerPoint cross the road? To get to the other slide.

Mom says Dad is so old at his party his candles cost more than the birthday cake!

How does the science teacher freshen her breath? With experi-mints!

I just got fired from the flower shop. Apparently, I took too many leaves.

Dad asked Mom, 'Do you find me dark and handsome?' She said, 'In the dark, I find you handsome!'

We all know why 6 was afraid of 7, but why was 19 afraid of 20? They had a fight, and 21.

How do you tune a fish? With its scales!

The moon had to get a haircut the other day. I heard eclipse it.

I didn't really enjoy my posh childhood. Everything was handed to me on a plate. Soup was a nightmare!

Mom insists she will meet Dad halfway in an argument - when he admits he's wrong, then she'll admit she's right!

What do you call a confused tree? Stumped.

Why did the bullfighter have to bring a giant mug of coffee before he could start his show? Because the animal he was faced with was a bull-dozer.

I built a car out of my old sports clothes. You could say it runs Lycra dream.

Shakespeare used to sell off-season camping gear. It was the winter of his discount tents!

Magicians aren't allowed to wear wigs for their performances. They have to keep their hare in their hat.

Mom says Dad is afraid of elevators. But he's taking steps to deal with it!

Traffic lights on my road have broken. No change there.

This bloke went to his doctor with a piece of lettuce sticking out of his arse. 'Ah yes,' said his doctor, 'that's just the tip of the Iceberg.'

Why are fart jokes so funny? They buttcrack you up!

Mom said she gets mad when somebody steals her utensils. Dad said that's a whisk he's willing to take!

What type of tea is the preferred choice for biologists? Reality.

Why do the French eat Snails? They don't like fast food.

What did one pen say to the other? You are incredible

What do history teachers talk about on dates? The good old days!

Dad once tried to eat a clock. He found it very time consuming!

A man who thinks he is a piece of luggage has been admitted to a hospital. Psychiatrists say he's the strangest case they've ever come across!

There was an inspirational song playing in the car that kept telling me to go the extra mile. Now I'm out of gas, and I don't know where I am.

I call my car Flattery – it gets me nowhere.

Accordion to a recent survey, inserting musical instruments randomly into sentences often goes unnoticed."

What's an alligator's favorite drink? Gatorade

Why did the two hamburgers not get along? Because they had beef.

Why was the chicken afraid of the chicken? It was chicken.

How do they teach reading at the North Pole Elementary School? They learn the elf-abet.

What do you call dinosaur eggs? Egnet

Which flower talks the most? Tulipe, because they have two lips.

Once on a field trip, I visited a prison library. It had prose and cons.

Why don't stairs like mirrors? No one likes being stared at!

Did you hear about the bankrupt poet? He ode everyone.

I recently finished building a model of Mount Everest. My daughter asked if it was to scale, but I had to say it wasn't. It was just for looking at.

Don't be irreplaceable - if you cannot be replaced, you cannot be promoted.

Why do bananas drag race? They love to peel out!

Be careful about trusting zombies. I hear they are rotten people!

What's the worst Dad joke ever? This one!

What do zombie kids do when their dads embarrass them? They roll their eyes.

I've been taking Viagra for my sunburn. It doesn't cure it, but during the night, it keeps the sheets off my legs.

Interesting fact of the day. A steak and kidney pie in Barbados will cost you £2.50, and a mince and onion pie in St Lucia will cost you £3.00.

My priest growing up, always wore a shirt that was torn while preaching. He said it was important to look holy.

What, I lost a finger? I asked the doctor, "Could I still write with that hand?" He said, "Probably. But I wouldn't count on it."

Over a century ago, two brothers from Dayton, Ohio, decided they could fly. They were Wright.

I've got a new job helping out a one-armed typist whenever she wants to do capital letters. It's shift work.

Did you hear about the little boy who was named after his father? His name is Dad.

Dad was fired from his job for making too many egg-jokes. He was laid off!

Mom says curse words are bad. Do you ever curse, Dad? "Of course not. I swear!"

Plan to be spontaneous...tomorrow.

Vampires are okay with smoking in bed, you know. They don't mind the coffin.

69% of people find something obscene in every sentence.

What do snowmen do on the weekend? Just chill.

What did the car say after it crashed? Ouch, that was wheely unfortunate.

What's a parasite? Something you see in Paris.

Have you seen the Gravity book I brought? I just can't seem to put it down.

What is black and terrible for the integrity of your teeth? A big rock.

Mom: Phones don't grow on trees! Then why are they called "Apple?"

That one goose refused to fly in formation. He was just winging it.

It was so cold today in the nation's capital that we got to see a politician put his hands in his own pockets for a change!

Dad said to Mom, "How come nobody ever listens to me?" She said, "Sorry, what was that?"

What do you call a road that's oddly elastic and springy? Highway rubbery.

Why does the crocodile with a sweet tooth love feasting on serpents? Because he loves eating pie thons.

I, for one, like Roman numerals.

What is the coldest letter? C, because it's in the middle of ice.

My son is studying to be a surgeon. I just hope he makes the cut.

Why was the fruit farmer leading such a lonely life? He was struggling to find dates.

What did the pirate's report card look like? He always got seven Cs.

Did you hear about the elf who got athletes' feet? Actually, what he got was mistletoe.

Why did the salmon finally break up with her narcissistic boyfriend? Because she finally got tired of how shellfish he was.

Ever heard the rope joke? Skip it.

Why did the hippie shark struggle to make friends with the seals? The seals struggled to believe he was from the Pacific.

I can't believe people don't believe the Earth is round. They must travel on a plane

What Jedi can you eat? Obi-Wan Cannoli!

My Dad said, 'starting tomorrow, whatever life throws at me, I'm ducking so it hits someone else.'

What form of public transport do mosquitoes take on their way to work? The public buzz.

Did you know that approximately 3.14% of sailors are pi-rates?

I don't mean to brag, but I finally made six figures last year. I was voted the worst employee at the model factory.

Why don't ghosts go into gyms? Because people are exorcising.

So I said to the train driver, 'I want to go to Paris.' He said, 'Eurostar?' I said, 'I can sing a bit, but I'm no Robbie Williams.'

Why should you not trust dermatologists? They make too many rash decisions.

Why is the Apple store so hot? Because they won't install Windows!

I've just started up an STD clinic from scratch.

What do jeans do to cool off in the summer? They start panting.

What do the guards who protect the royal family love to do in their spare time? Guard-ening.

A fake noodle? That thing is an impasta!

If I could do anything in this life, I would like to clean mirrors. It's something I've always been able to see myself doing.

My doctor told me I was turning into an airport. I said, 'Is it terminal?'

My wife is never going to send me grocery shopping again. She only asked for six cans of sprite from the store, but I just realized I picked 7 up.

What runs faster, cold or hot? Hot, because you can catch a cold!

Melons always have weddings. It's too bad they cantaloupe.

Why did the web developer cross the road? TO GET to the other ride.

I'm working on a joke about immortality. I really hope it never gets old.

Boycott shampoo! Demand the real poo.

My nasal congestion is getter better. It 'snot so bad today!

I went to a urologist who told me I needed a cystoscopy. I asked him what's that? He said, 'we're going to Youtube your Peetube!'

What kind of self-help books do dolphins read? Leading a porpoise-driven life

What do you call underwear in a storm? Thunderpants

That bike has had trouble standing up on its own. My guess is because it is two tired.

Why was the chimpanzee unable to enter his apartment after a long night of drinking with his other fellow primates? He could not find his monkey.

Have you ever heard of how crazy a squirrel's diet is? Most will say it's nuts.

Conjunctivitis.com. That's a site for sore eyes.

My friend is an amazing soap opera singer. She sings opera in the shower, and sometimes soap falls in her mouth.

A train stops at a train station. A bus stops at a bus station. Now why is my desk called a 'work station'?

This chicken came up to me and said, 'I can't find my eggs.' I said, 'You've probably mislaid them.'

My wife left me because of how I can't stop talking about pasta. Now I'm feeling canneloni.

What did one shipwreck say to another? I've got a sinking feeling.

Trying to pin a man down can be like trying to nail blancmange.

My first time in an elevator was an uplifting experience. The second time let me down.

How do hurricanes see? With one eye

I can't decide which of these knots is better. I guess it's a tie.

What do dentists call their x-rays? Tooth pics!

What kind of keys can't unlock doors? Monkeys!

Why did the mummy run away when it was his turn to sing at the open mic night? Because he had no guts!

Why did the cow cross the road? To get to the moooooovies.

Making a new password: ME: beefstew. COMPUTER: Sorry, password not stroganoff.

What's Bunny's favorite game? Hopscotch

Nostalgia isn't what it used to be.

I'm a lawyer, and my wife and I got in a fight recently because she was fed up with my very particular brand of humor.

What animal is constantly wearing hats because it is very self-conscious of its hairline? The bald eagle.

What did the toilet-paper roll complain about? "People just keep ripping me off!"

Dogs eat almost anything, especially bones. Never a trombone, though.

As a family, we couldn't decide whether to have our granny cremated or buried, so in the end, we let her live.

I usually meet my boyfriend at 12:59 because I like that one-to-one time.

When they're younger, arboretums are actually elementree schools.

Why do vampires have no friends? They suck.

The color green makes it hard to find a partner. It's always single, and I think it's because it is always so jaded.

I entered a competition putting sails on boats. It was rigged.

What was the coffee's motto? Espresso sele.

I'm currently reading a book called 'My Life' by Bill Clinton. It freaked me out. I didn't think he knew anything about me.

I watched hockey before. It was cool. It was swimming. I watched swimming.

Every day I tell my wife I'm going to jog around the neighborhood, but I never do. It's a running joke, I have.

Who helps coffee understand how to be more British? His TEA-cher.

Dad says his favorite pen can write underwater. It can write other words as well, but underwater is one of his favorites!

What did the llama say before his vacation? Alpaca bag.

Peter Pan just keeps flying around and around. He neverlands!

I'm very proud of the English educational system we have today. It's by far the goodest in the world.

Why was the painting incarcerated for a crime it never committed? It was framed!

I sold my guitar today to a bloke with no arms. I asked how it was going to work, and he said, 'I play by ear.'

I got robbed on an elevator. That was wrong on so many levels!

I live in an airport, but when the security guard comes at night, Heathrows me out.

What goes through every village, over mountains, crosses rivers and deserts, and yet never moves? A road.

What's the karate expert's favorite beverage? Karatea

What did the daddy water bottle say to the baby water bottle? Come here, squirt!

What did a pitcher say to the volcano? Batter erupt

What's brown and runs round a field? A fence.

What time does the elf like to eat? Elfven o'clock

Why did the ice cream and milk become friends? Because they wanted to shake things up!

Why did the pig take a bath? Because the farmer said, "Hogwash!"

Why are telescopes pointed away from Earth? Because they search for intelligent life

Do you know those people who make calendars? They can never take a day off.

What has a bottom at its top? Aley.

What was the turtle trying to convince his teacher when he arrived late to class? That he didn't arrive late on porpoise.

Why was Santa's tiny helper feeling depressed? Because he had low elf-esteem.

Are you from Starbucks? Because I like you a latte.

Dad gave up his job repairing crystal balls. He couldn't see a future in it.

A boiled egg is hard to beat.

Everything you've ever thought about was about potatoes or not about potatoes.

Where do mailmen go on vacation? Parcelona!

Why do seafood restaurant chefs always end up single? Because they are shellfish lovers!

Biggest Cause of road rage? Crossroads.

Why did you buy the new hedge trimmer? Because it's cutting hedge technology.

People who get abducted by extraterrestrials can't really tell anyone. They must feel so alienated.

I'm a three-times-a-night man. That toilet light is hardly ever off.

I'm studying anthropology. I went to my local library and said, 'Do you keep books on pygmies?' The girl said, 'No, only on shelves.'

Dad, I made a cheese board. Maybe you should tell the cheese more interesting stories then.

This spaceship landed in front of me, and out of it stepped a 5-metre diameter cream bun. It was one of those extra cholesterols.

Why did the algebra textbook have to make an urgent appointment with a therapist? Because he was full of problems.

I just saw a box of After Eights on eBay. Mint condition.

Why do calendars always pay for their dates? Because it's on them.

Those who jump off into the Paris river are in Seine.

Mom says Dad was born upside down, his nose runs, and his feet smell!

I can't remember the name of my homing pigeon, but I'm sure it'll come back to me.

The soap Casualty is now in its twenty-sixth year. Ironically, it's not getting any better.

I've spilled stain remover on my trousers. How do I get that out?

Why do bears have hairy coats? Fur protection.

That picture should never have gotten arrested—it was framed!

Dentistry can be such a depressing job. You're always looking down in the mouth.

What do history teachers talk about when they're attracted to each other? Dates!

Dad told Mom she should embrace her mistakes. So she gave him a big hug!

I saw this film about prehistoric pigs – Jurassic Pork'.

Why should you avoid people dressed as celery? They could be stalking you!

There's a new surgeon in town who does quick surgeries on insects. I even heard he did one on the fly.

On what side of the house do trees grow best? The outside

What did the dying composer say? I'll be Bach.

How does a lawyer say goodbye? I'll be suing ya!

Mom says Dad is so old his back goes out more than he does!

What happens to a pig when it spends too much time in the hot sun? It stars bacon.

When Hurricane Ian came through, I lost about 25% of my whole roof. Oof.

Where does a horse go when it's injured? To the horsepital!

I just went to an emotional wedding. Even the cake was in tiers.

I went to the store to find a camouflage jack... I couldn't find one.

Why do oranges hate the police? They are always getting squeezed for information.

We were at a wedding last weekend, and it was so beautiful. Even the cake was in tiers.

Why was the civil engineer's relationship so unstable? Because there was no truss left!

Did you hear about the light bulb party? It was pretty lit.

Why was the strawberry late? He was caught in a jam.

Why do cows eat from round hay bales? Because they don't like to eat square meals!

It was very unfortunate to hear about the cheesemonger that caught fire last week in Paris. Apparently, all that was left was de brie.

Dijon vu - the same mustard as before.

What do noses say instead of goodbye? Smell you later!

What did the art teacher yell at his students after leaping out from behind the door during Halloween to scare them? Supplies!

I keep trying to lose weight, but it always finds me.

Did you see the horse that could balance a corncob on its head? It was some unique corn.

How do you make a room warm? By giving it a second coat.

Recently I went fell walking in the Lake District. That's not strictly true. I actually fell, walking in the Lake District.

Just came back from a mind reader. I can't get her off my head.

Dad says Forrest Gump's computer password is
1forrest1

Q: Why did the nose want to stay home from school?
A: He was tired of getting picked on.

An archaeologist. Someone whose career lies in ruins.

30 million acres of rainforest are being destroyed every year, and here I am attempting to recycle a single jar of Marmite.

A jump lead walked into a bar. The barman said, 'I'll serve you, but don't start anything.'

Opera enthusiasts are the Fandom of the Opera.

Trees never have a problem accessing the web. They can always log on.

I do portraits of boxers. I can knock them out really quickly.

Dad entered what he'd eaten today into his fitness app, and it sent an ambulance to the house!

What's brown and sounds like a bell? Dung!

I finally found the perfect way to fix procrastination, But I'll have to tell you later.

What do you call two chimpanzees who share the same Amazon account? Prime-mates!

We had a huge renovation project for our home. The first floor was going well, but now the upstairs? It's a whole other story.

I thought I'd pour beer over my garden before planting the lawn. I hoped it would come up half-cut.

A prisoner with a stutter died in prison......before he could finish his sentence.

Batman walks into a superhero-only pool, and he is quickly stopped by a guard; the guard points to a sign that says, "No swimming without supervision."

Why do ghouls and ghosts like to go in elevators? Because they like to raise their spirits.

I bought a book on DIY. So far, my dad has read me a hundred-three pages of it.

Why is Dracula so unpopular? He's a pain in the neck.

Ed has no girlfriend, as Sheeran away.

I started following Vin Diesel on Instagram. He's a tough actor to follow!

'Dad, are we pyromaniacs?' 'We arson.'

Why did Dad buy a universal remote? Because it changes everything.

I'd have a coffee, but it's not my cup of tea.

I painted a picture of my cat's feet today. You could say it was a paw-trait.

Need an ark? INoah guy.

Could you please open the jam container? Why? It's already a jar.

Why couldn't the shoes go out to play? They were all tied up!

This is your captain waking. AND THIS IS YOUR CAPTAIN SHOUTING.

When he's bored, Dad rings Best Western Hotels, and when they reply with 'Best Western.' He answers, 'True Grit with John Wayne.' Then roars with laughter.

Did you hear about the school that converted to Marxism? I heard they don't have any classes.

What did the doctor tell the patient who said he thought his eyes were changing color? 'It's just a pigment of your imagination!'

What do you call a lost wolf? A where-wolf!

What's a cow's favorite color? Blooooo!

Mom says 'Dad is so old that a fireman has to be in attendance every time he lights his birthday candles!"

What do you call a pharmacist that helps everyone? Piller of the community.

Who was the most famous animal artist? Pigassol

I never thought my brother would try to steal my job as a road worker. Then I started seeing the signs.

Never play leapfrog with a unicorn or a porcupine.

What do you call the Spanish translation of the Star Wars spin-off movie? Rogue Juan.

The patient said, 'Can I administer my own anesthetic?' The surgeon replied, 'Go ahead, knock yourself out!'

Why did the policeman give his young son a fine for not going to bed on time? Because he was resisting a rest.

Children shouldn't watch big band performances on TV-too much sax and violins.

Why do dogs run in circles? Because it's hard to run in squares!

What do you call a white bucket? Pail.

Mom says Dad is so old they've canceled his blood type!

Did you hear about the pirate who decided to learn how to become a chef instead of spending his time terrorizing Neverland? Captain Cook.

The supermarket checkout sign said, 'Eight items or less.' So, I changed my name to Les.

Why is it impossible to know when a psychiatrist goes to the bathroom? Because the "P" is silent.

For a while in my college days, I got addicted to soap. Don't worry, I'm clean now.

Dad said he would buy me a telescope since I was so interested in astronomy. I said I'd look into it!

When do doctors get angry? When they run out of patients.

My wife left me because of all the overtime I'm doing as a security guard at the airport. As she walked out, I said, 'Did you pack your own bags?"

What did the flame tell his parents when he fell in love? I've found the perfect match!

I can't believe that the penguin was denied bail. He's not even a flight risk!

Why do kangaroos love koalas? Because they have many fine koalaties!

What do you do to dead chemists? Your barium.

Why was the horse so happy? Because he lived in a stable environment.

My son didn't tell me he ate some glue. His lips were sealed.

30% of car accidents in Sweden involve a moose. I say don't let them drive.

Do mascara and lipstick ever argue? Sure, but then they makeup.

The night club nearby recently contracted a carpenter. He's really tearing up the dance floor.

What do you call Garfield's uncle? Garfuncle

Made in the USA
Columbia, SC
22 December 2024